Air Fryer Cookbook for Two

101 Low-Fat Recipes for Beginners and Pros to Grill, Fry and Bake Most Delicious Meals with Less Oil

Ann Brown

1

Table of Contents

TABLE OF CONTENTS 4

INTRODUCTION 7

AIR FRYER COOKING OVERVIEW 9

BENEFITS OF AIR FRYER COOKING 10

ESTIMATED COOKING TIME CHART 12

COOKING MEASUREMENT CONVERSION CHART 13

BREAKFAST RECIPES 15

Quick & Easy Toasted Cheese 15
Easy Springs Rolls 16
Breakfast Egg Muffins with Sausage and Toasts 17
Delicious Cheesy Omelet 18
Morning Cheesy Risotto 19
Breakfast Cinnamon Toasts 20
Classic English Breakfast 21
Avocado with Eggs 22
Amazing Breakfast Muffins 23
Breakfast Frittata 24

DELICIOUS LUNCH AND DINNER RECIPES 25

Air Fryer Sriracha Cauliflower 25
Turkey Risotto 26
Baked Sweet Potatoes 27
Delicious Crispy Air Fried Pickles 28
Easy Air Fried Falafel 29
Savory Air Fryer Potato Croquettes 30
Unusual Kale and Potato Nuggets 31
Air Fried Zucchini Crisps 32

AIR FRYER SNACK AND APPETIZER RECIPES 33

Mutton Chops 33
Easy and Quick Banana Chips 34
Tortilla Chips 35
Delicious Potato Chips 36
Grilled Broccoli 37
Broccoli Pesto with Quinoa 38
Cauliflower Gratin 39

MOUTH-WATERING SIDE AIR FRYER RECIPES..40

AIR FRYER POTATO CHIPS 40
FLAVORFUL GARLIC POTATOES WITH TURKEY 41
GARLIC STUFFED MUSHROOMS..42
ROASTED POTATOES AND YOGHURT 43
ROASTED POTATOES WITH ROSEMARY 44
CHEESY RICE BALLS 45
CLASSIC FRENCH FRIES..46
DELICIOUS GRILLED CHEESE 47
ROASTED BRUSSELS SPROUTS 48
TURKEY WRAPPED PRAWNS 49
WALNUT STILTON CIRCLES 50

AIR FRYER FISH AND SEAFOOD RECIPES..51

CRISPY AIR FRYER CATFISH 51
DELICIOUS CAJUN SHRIMP 52
AIR FRYER CRISPY CRUST FISH FILLETS 53
AIR FRIED SALMON CROQUETTES 54
EASY AIR FRYER FISH STRIPS 55
AIR FRIED COD NUGGETS 56
CRISPY AIR FRIED SHRIMP 57
CREAMY AIR FRYER SALMON 58
AIR FRIED CRAB HERB CROQUETTES 59
SUPER CHEESY BREADED SALMON 60
PARMESAN-CRUSTED TILAPIA 61

AIR FRYER POULTRY RECIPES..62

CHICKEN NUGGETS 62
CRISPY CHICKEN DRUMSTICKS..63
FLAVORFUL CURRY CHICKEN 64
GARLIC LEMON CHICKEN 65
DELICIOUS BACON WRAPPED CHICKEN................................66
SPICY CHICKEN WINGS 67
ROASTED WHOLE CHICKEN WITH HERBS 68
HERB ORANGE CHICKEN WINGS 69
BUFFALO WINGS 70
EASY TERIYAKI CHICKEN 71

AIR FRYER PORK AND LAMB RECIPES..72

SWEET AND SOUR DELICIOUS PORK 72
CHAR SIU 73
COUNTRY FRIED STEAK 74
EASY COOKING PORK CHOP 75
PORK SATAY WITH PEANUT SAUCE 76
ZERO OIL PORK CHOPS 77
DELICIOUS PORK TENDERLOIN..78

DRUNKEN HAM WITH MUSTARD 79
SPICY LAMB CHOPS 80
GRILLED VEGETABLES WITH LAMB 81
CARROT LAMB MEATBALLS 82
LAMB CHOPS WITH GARLIC SAUCE 83
DELICIOUS LAMB PATTIES 84

AIR FRYER BEEF RECIPES 85

SIMPLE AIR FRIED BEEF STEAK 85
CRISPY CRUST BEEF SCHNITZEL 86
AMAZINGLY EASY AIR FRYER MEATLOAF 87
STUFFED BELL PEPPER 88
MARINATED BEEF AND BROCCOLI 89
DELICIOUS CHEESY BURGER PATTIES 90
SWEET AND TANGY MEATBALLS 91
AIR FRIED ROAST BEEF 92
CRISPY BEEF CUBES 93
BEEF STEAK 94

AIR FRYER VEGETABLE RECIPES 95

BALSAMIC ARTICHOKES 95
BEET SALAD AND PARSLEY DRESSING 96
BEETS AND BLUE CHEESE SALAD 97
BEET, TOMATO AND GOAT CHEESE MIX 98
BROCCOLI SALAD 99
BRUSSELS SPROUTS AND TOMATOES MIX 100
SPICY FRIED CABBAGE 101
SWEET BABY CARROTS 102
HERBED EGGPLANT AND ZUCCHINI MIX 103
FLAVORED FENNEL 104

AIR FRYER DESSERT RECIPES 105

EASY PINEAPPLE STICKS 105
BANANA OATS COOKIES 106
CRISP AND SWEET BANANAS 107
DOUBLE CHOCOLATE CHIP COOKIES 108
BLUEBERRY PANCAKES 109
CHOCOLATE MOLTEN LAVA CAKE 110
ROASTED PUMPKIN SEEDS WITH CINNAMON 111
APPLE WEDGES WITH CINNAMON 112
FRIED BANANAS WITH ICE CREAM 113
LITTLE APPLE PIE 114
CHOCOLATE MUG CAKE 115

CONCLUSION 116

Introduction

First of all I want to thank you so much for buying my book: Air Fryer Cookbook for Two: 101 Low-Fat Recipes for Beginners and Pros to Grill, Fry and Bake Most Delicious Meals with Less Oil. In this book I tried to collect the most delicious and at the same time the easiest dishes for Air Fryer so that you could cook amazing fried and low-fat dishes for two.

Among the more than 100 recipes you can find quick breakfast recipes, lunches and dinners, meat, poultry, fish and seafood recipes. The book also contains plenty of snack, appetizers and vegetable dishes. I tried not to avoid desserts too - I have specially collected for you the best desserts that can be cooked in air fryer.

All the recipes in this book contain a list of necessary ingredients. It should be noted that each recipe is designed for 2 people, but if you have a family dinner or a party for your best friends, you can easily cook your favorite dish just by increasing the amount of ingredients. For example, if you need to cook for 4 people, just double the amount of food. Also, if you're cooking meatballs, for example, and you've decided to increase your meal size, just prepare them in two batches so that you don't overload the air fryer.

This cookbook contains recipes that are suitable for both beginners and pros. Just follow the directions in each recipe and you will get tasty and healthy low fat meals.

I'm sure you'll enjoy my recipes. So, unpack your air fryer, clean it and let's get started!

Air Fryer Cooking Overview

You'll ask - so what is air fryer?

Air Fryer is a special kitchen appliance that allows you to cook fried food with a low fat content. The principle of operation of air fryer is to circulate hot air at high speed. This allows you to cook traditional fried dishes with low fat. In particular, manufacturers claim that the amount of fat in the dishes is on average reduced by 50-75% compared to traditional frying methods.

Not all air fryers cook at the same speed. All of them differ from each other in size and power - which directly affects the time of cooking. One thing remains unchanged - high speed, convenience and incredible taste of cooked fried meals.

Benefits of Air Fryer Cooking

In addition to the advantages described above, air fryer has several other benefits that make this kitchen appliance incredibly effective and literally master-have appliance

Low Fat Cooking

Perhaps, the most valuable advantage of air fryer is that it provides you with a finished product that is very similar to the usual fried food, with minimal fat. Due to the classic frying methods a large amount of oil is used, which provides crispy crust, but at the same time - more harmful fat and extra calories.

With the air fryer you can cook your favorite fried meals, such as French fries or fried chicken wings with the same crispy crust and low fat.

Safety cooking

Unlike traditional frying, where hot oil sprays in all directions and you have plenty of ways to burn yourself, cooking in air fryer is completely safe. This device does not have outdoor areas where you can accidentally get burned.

Quickly warms up

A distinctive feature of air fryer is the rapid heating of the device. Usually it takes only 2-3 minutes to reach the required temperature and start cooking.

Variety of cooking

Thanks to air fryer you can cook a huge amount of dishes depending on your wishes. For example, you can cook ribs, vegetable dishes, beef, pork or lamb. Moreover, you can prepare a variety of desserts, such as fruit chips, pies, fruit bread and many other delicious and healthy food. By the way, air fryer can easily replace some traditional kitchen appliances and become indispensable in your kitchen.

Easy to clean
Most kitchen appliances require a lot of effort to clean them after cooking. But not air fryer. You won't have any problems with this appliance. Not only cook quickly but it also cleans quickly. Once it has cooled down, you can disassemble the air fryer for spare parts and put them in the dishwasher. Also, due to the minimal use of oil during cooking, the parts of the oven are not very dirty, which allows you to wash the device in minutes.

Estimated Cooking Time Chart

Type	Food	Cooking Time	Temperature (Fahrenheit)
Fish	Breaded Shrimp	9 minutes	400
Fish	Fish Fillet	10-12 minutes	380-400
Fish	Frozen Fish Fillets	14 minutes	400
Fish	Scallops	5-7 minutes	400
Fish	Shrimp	6 minutes	400
Meat	Bacon	5-7 minutes	400
Meat	Beef Roast	45-50 minutes	390
Meat	Chicken Breast, boneless	12 minutes	380
Meat	Chicken Breast, with bone	25 minutes	370
Meat	Chicken Nuggets	12 minutes	390
Meat	Chicken Tenders	10 minutes	360
Meat	Chicken Wings	12 minutes	400
Meat	Fillet Mignon	18 minutes	400
Meat	Flank Steak	12 minutes	400
Meat	Game Hen	20 minutes	390
Meat	Hamburger	15-20 minutes	370
Meat	Lamb Chops	10 minutes	400
Meat	Meatballs	7 minutes	380
Meat	Pork Chops, bone in	12 minutes	400
Meat	Pork Loin	50 minutes	360
Meat	Pork Tenderloin	15 minutes	370
Meat	Rack of Lamb	20 minutes	380
Meat	Sausage	15 minutes	380
Meat	T-Bone Steak	10-15 minutes	380
Meat	Whole Chicken	60-75 minutes	360
Sides	Mozzarella Sticks	8 minutes	400
Sides	Onion Rings	8 minutes	400
Sides	Thin French Fries	15 minutes	390
Vegetable	Asparagus	5 minutes	400
Vegetable	Broccoli	6 minutes	400
Vegetable	Brussels Sprouts	15 minutes	380
Vegetable	Cauliflower	12 minutes	400
Vegetable	Potatoes, whole	40 minutes	400
Vegetable	Sweet Potatoes	30 minutes	380
Vegetable	Zucchini	12 minutes	350

Cooking Measurement Conversion Chart

Liquid Measures

1 gal = 4 qt = 8 pt = 16 cups = 128 fl oz
½ gal = 2 qt = 4 pt = 8 cups = 64 fl oz
¼ gal = 1 qt = 2 pt = 4 cups = 32 fl oz
½ qt = 1 pt = 2 cups = 16 fl oz
¼ qt = ½ pt = 1 cup = 8 fl oz

Dry Measures

1 cup = 16 Tbsp = 48 tsp = 250ml
¾ cup = 12 Tbsp = 36 tsp = 175ml
⅔ cup = 10 ⅔ Tbsp = 32 tsp = 150ml
½ cup = 8 Tbsp = 24 tsp = 125ml
⅓ cup = 5 ⅓ Tbsp = 16 tsp = 75ml
¼ cup = 4 Tbsp = 12 tsp = 50ml
⅛ cup = 2 Tbsp = 6 tsp = 30ml
1 Tbsp = 3 tsp = 15ml

Dash or Pinch or Speck = less than ⅛ tsp

Quickies

1 fl oz = 30 ml
1 oz = 28.35 g
1 lb = 16 oz (454 g)
1 kg = 2.2 lb
1 quart = 2 pints

U.S.	Canadian
¼ tsp	1.25 mL
½ tsp	2.5 mL
1 tsp	5 mL
1 Tbl	15 mL
¼ cup	50 mL
⅓ cup	75 mL
½ cup	125 mL
⅔ cup	150 mL
¾ cup	175 mL
1 cup	250 mL
1 quart	1 liter

Recipe Abbreviations

Cup = c or C
Fluid = fl
Gallon = gal
Ounce = oz
Package = pkg
Pint = pt
Pound = lb or #
Quart = qt
Square = sq
Tablespoon = T or Tbl
    or TBSP or TBS
Teaspoon = t or tsp

Fahrenheit (°F) to Celcius (°C)

$$°C = (°F - 32) \times 5/9$$

°F	°C
32 °F	0 °C
40 °F	4 °C
140 °F	60 °C
150 °F	65 °C
160 °F	70 °C
225 °F	107 °C
250 °F	121 °C
275 °F	135 °C
300 °F	150 °C
325 °F	165 °C
350 °F	177 °C
375 °F	190 °C
400 °F	205 °C
425 °F	220 °C
450 °F	230 °C
475 °F	245 °C
500 °F	260 °C

OVEN TEMPERATURES

WARMING: 200 °F
VERY SLOW: 250 °F - 275 °F
SLOW: 300 °F - 325 °F
MODERATE: 350 °F - 375 °F
HOT: 400 °F - 425 °F
VERY HOT: 450 °F - 475 °F

*Some measurements were rounded

Breakfast Recipes

Quick & Easy Toasted Cheese

- Ready in 20 minutes
- Servings: 2

Ingredients

- 2 sliced white bread
- 4 oz cheese on your preference, grated
- 1 tsp butter

Directions

1. Firstly, cook the bread in the toaster.
2. Preheat the air fryer to 350F. Once toasted, spread the butter on bread pieces. Cover with grated cheese.
3. Place covered bread slices into the Fryer and cook for 4-6 minutes.
4. Serve with your favorite sauce and enjoy.

Easy Springs Rolls

- Ready in 40 minutes
- Servings: 2

Ingredients

- 1 cup mince of any kind
- 1 small onion, diced
- 1 packet spring rolls
- 2 oz Asian noodles
- 1 clove garlic, crushed
- 1/2 cup mixed vegetables
- 1 tbsp sesame oil
- 2 tbsp water
- Salt and pepper, to taste

Directions

1. First of all, prepare the noodles: let them soak in the hot water. When they are soft enough, cut them and set aside. Take the wok and grease it with sesame oil and heat.
2. When it is hot, add mince, vegetables, onion, and crushed garlic. Season with salt and cook over medium-high heat stirring often until the mince is cooked through. It may take 3-5 minutes if you are using wok, and 7-10 minutes if you are using a regular frying pan.
3. Stir through the noodles. Leave it and wait for the juices to be absorbed.
4. Take a spring roll sheet, add a strip of filling diagonally across.
5. Fold the top point over the filling. Then fold in both the side points.
6. Before rolling the spring roll over the final point brush it with cold water to seal it. Do the same to all other spring roll sheets.
7. Preheat the air fryer to 340F.
8. Lightly sprinkle spring rolls with oil and transfer them to the air fryer. Cook for about 6-8 minutes, then serve.

Breakfast Egg Muffins with Sausage and Toasts

- Ready in 30 minutes
- Servings: 2

Ingredients

- ¼ cup skimmed milk
- 2 sausages, boiled
- 3 large eggs
- 1 piece of bread, sliced lengthwise
- 4 tbsp grated cheese
- Salt and black pepper, to taste
- Chopped fresh herbs for seasoning

Directions

1. Preheat the air fryer to 360F
2. Meanwhile, break the eggs into a large bowl and whisk them with milk.
3. Take 2 muffin cups and grease them with a cooking spray. Pour the equal amount of egg mixture into each of them.
4. Arrange sliced sausages with bread slices in muffin cups, sinking them deeply into the egg and milk mixture. Sprinkle with cheese and add a bit of salt to taste.
5. Put the muffin cups into the Air Fryer and set the timer for 15-20 minutes, depending on the consistency you prefer.
6. When almost ready, sprinkle muffins with chopped herbs you prefer.

Delicious Cheesy Omelet

- Ready in 25 minutes
- Servings: 2

Ingredients

- 1 medium onion, chopped
- 4 tbsp cheddar cheese, grated
- 3 large eggs
- ½ tsp soy sauce
- Salt to taste
- Ground black pepper, to taste
- Cooking spray

Directions

1. In a large mixing bowl, combine together eggs, salt, pepper, and soy sauce. Whisk well.
2. Preheat the air fryer to 360F.
3. Spray a small pan, which fits inside the air fryer with cooking spray. Add onions and spread it all over the pan and place the pan inside the air fryer. Cook for 6-7 minutes or until onions are translucent.
4. Pour the beaten egg mixture all over the onions. Sprinkle cheese all over it. Air fry for another 5-6 minutes.
5. Remove from the Air Fryer and serve with toasted multi grain bread.

Morning Cheesy Risotto

- Ready in 40 minutes
- Servings: 2

Ingredients

- 1 small onion, diced
- 2 cups chicken stock, boiling
- ½ cup parmesan cheese or cheddar cheese, grated
- 1 clove garlic, minced
- ¾ cup arborio rice
- 1 tbsp olive oil
- 1 tbsp butter, unsalted
- Salt and pepper, to taste

Directions

1. Preheat the air fryer to 390F.
2. Grease round baking tin with oil and add stirring the butter, onion, and garlic. Place the tin into the air fryer and cook for about 5 minutes. Then add rice and cook for another 4 minutes. Stir three times during the cooking time.
3. Reduce the heat to 320F and set the timer to 20 minutes. Pour in the chicken stock and stir gently. Do not cover the air fryer.
4. Add in the cheese, stir once again and serve.

Breakfast Cinnamon Toasts

- Ready in 15 minutes
- Servings: 2

Ingredients

- 4 bread slices
- 2 tbsp salted butter
- 1 tbsp sugar
- 1 tsp ground cinnamon
- ½ tsp vanilla extract

Directions

1. In a large mixing bowl combine salted butter, sugar, cinnamon, and vanilla extract. Mix to combine well.
2. Spread the mixture over bread slices.
3. Preheat the air fryer to 380F and place bread slices to a fryer.
4. Cook for 4-5 minutes and serve hot!

Classic English Breakfast

- Ready in 35 minutes
- Servings: 2

Ingredients

- 2 large eggs
- 2 medium-sized potatoes
- 1 sausage
- 2 toasts
- 2 cups beans in tomato sauce
- 1 cup sliced and diced potatoes
- 1 tbsp olive oil
- Salt to taste

Directions

1. Preheat your air fryer to 390F. Crack the eggs onto an oven safe dish. Sprinkle with salt if desired. Place the beans next to the eggs.
2. In a separate container, place the potatoes, and 1 tablespoon of olive oil, combine well. Sprinkle with salt if desired.
3. First place the potatoes in the Air Fryer. Cook for 10 minutes. Then place the form with the eggs and the beans. Cover the potatoes with parchment paper to separate. Cook for an additional 10 minutes.
4. Cut the sausage into pieces and add to the dish with the beans and eggs. Cook for another 5 minutes.
5. Serve with toast and coffee for a big and hearty breakfast.

Avocado with Eggs

- Ready in 15 minutes
- Servings: 2

Ingredients

- 1 large avocado, sliced
- 1/2 cup of panko bread crumbs
- ½ cup of flour
- 2 eggs, beaten
- ¼ tsp of paprika
- Black pepper and salt, to taste

Directions

1. Preheat the air fryer 400F.
2. Season the avocado slices with some salt and pepper.
3. Dust the avocados with some flour and dip them in the eggs then roll them in the breadcrumbs.
4. Place the avocado slices in the air fryer then fry for 6 minutes.

Amazing Breakfast Muffins

- Ready in 25 minutes
- Servings: 2

Ingredients

- 2 small eggs, whisked
- 2 tbsp vegetable oil
- ½ cup milk
- 1 cup plain flour
- 1 tbsp baking powder
- ½ tsp of mustard powder
- 2 oz Parmesan, grated
- 1 tsp Worcestershire sauce
- 2 tomatoes, for garnishing
- A Handful of basil leaves for garnishing

Directions

1. Preheat the air fryer to 390F. Combine two muffin cases to form one. Take a large bowl and whisk the egg in it. Pour in milk and oil. Add in the baking powder and flour. Combine it to form a smooth paste.
2. Add Parmesan cheese, mustard powder and Worcestershire sauce. Mix well and then fill the muffin cups with the mixture.
3. Cook in the air fryer for about 15 minutes. Then arrange the muffins in the muffin tray and garnish with slices of tomato and basil leaves.

Breakfast Frittata

- Ready in 15 minutes
- Servings: medium frittata for 2 persons

Ingredients

- 4 cherry tomatoes, sliced into halves
- 3 eggs
- ½ Italian sausage
- 1 tbsp olive oil
- 4 tbsp parmesan cheese, grated
- Parsley, chopped
- Salt and pepper, to taste

Directions

1. Preheat the air fryer to 360F.
2. Put the sausage and cherry tomato halves into a baking accessory that will fit in your air fryer basket. Fry for nearly 5 minutes.
3. Beat the eggs into a medium bowl, add the remaining ingredients, and whisk until combined.
4. Carefully open the air fryer drawer and remove the baking accessory.
5. Pour the egg mixture into baking accessory and evenly distribute. Return into the air fryer basket and then bake for 5 minutes.
6. Serve and enjoy.

Delicious Lunch and Dinner Recipes

Air Fryer Sriracha Cauliflower

- Ready in 25 minutes
- Servings: 4

Ingredients

- 2 tbsp butter, melted
- ¼ cup sriracha sauce
- 4 cups cauliflower florets
- 1 cup panko bread crumbs
- A pinch of salt and black pepper, to taste

Directions

1. In a large mixing bowl, combine together butter and sriracha sauce.
2. Pour over the cauliflower florets and toss to coat. In another bowl, mix the breadcrumbs and salt.
3. Preheat the air fryer to 360F.
4. Dip the cauliflower florets in the panko mixture and place inside the air fryer. Cook for 15-20 until cooked.

Turkey Risotto

- Ready in 1 hour 30 minutes
- Servings: 2

Ingredients

- 1 medium onion, chopped
- 1 can (8 oz) mushroom, drained
- 3 cups stock, either vegetable or turkey
- 1 cups turkey, chopped
- 1 cups beer
- 1 cup risotto rice
- ½ cup parmesan cheese, grated
- 2 tbsp olive oil, divided
- 1 tbsp butter
- 1 tsp basil, dried
- 1 tsp oregano, dried

Directions

1. In a large stock pot, boil the stock and then set it aside.
2. Chop the onion. In a large bowl mix the onion with 1 tbsp olive oil.
3. Preheat the air fryer to 320F and cook onion for about 3-5 minutes, stirring often.
4. Add the drained mushrooms, oregano and basil to the air fryer basket with the precooked onions. Cook the mixture for another 10 minutes. In the warmed mixture, add the final tablespoon of extra virgin olive oil, as well as the risotto rice.
5. Cook the mixture for 5 more minutes. Add the beer, and then cook for another 5 minutes.
6. Add the turkey and hot stock, and cook for 25 minutes.
7. Finally, add the butter and grated parmesan cheese, and cook for a final 5 minutes. This should be cooked al dente.
8. Serve immediately with a sprinkle of grated parmesan cheese.

Baked Sweet Potatoes

- Ready in 55 minutes
- Servings: 2

Ingredients

- 2 medium sweet potatoes, peeled and cubed
- 2 carrots, cut into chunks
- 2 cups broccoli florets
- 1 zucchini, sliced thickly
- Salt and pepper, to taste
- ¼ cup olive oil
- 1 tbsp onion powder

Directions

1. Preheat the air fryer to 400F.
2. In a baking dish that can fit inside the air fryer, mix all the ingredients and bake for 45 minutes or until the vegetables are tender and the sides have browned.

Delicious Crispy Air Fried Pickles

- Ready in 30 minutes
- Servings: 2

Ingredients

- 6 dill pickles, sliced
- ¼ cup all-purpose flour
- 1/8 tsp baking powder
- A pinch of salt
- 2 tbsp cornstarch + 3 tbsp water
- 6 tbsp panko breadcrumbs
- ½ tsp paprika
- Cooking spray

Directions

1. Dry the pickles using a paper towel then set aside.
2. In a large bowl, mix together the all-purpose flour, baking powder and salt.
3. Add the cornstarch and water slurry. Whisk until well combined.
4. Place the panko breadcrumbs in a shallow bowl or plate and add paprika. Mix until combined.
5. Dredge the pickles in the flour batter first then on to the panko.
6. Place on a plate and spray all pickles with oil.
7. Preheat the air fryer to 390F and cook for 15 minutes or until golden brown.

Easy Air Fried Falafel

- Ready in 30 minutes
- Servings: 2

Ingredients

- 1/2 tsp cumin seeds
- ½ tsp coriander seeds
- 1 cup chickpeas from can, drained and rinsed
- ½ tsp red pepper flakes
- 1 garlic clove, minced
- 1 tbsp parsley, chopped
- 1 tbsp coriander, chopped
- ½ onion, diced
- 1 tbsp juice from freshly squeezed lemon
- 3 tbsp all-purpose flour
- ½ tsp salt
- Cooking spray

Directions

1. In a skillet over medium heat, toast the cumin and coriander seeds until fragrant.
2. Place the toasted seeds in a mortar and grind the seeds. In a food processor, place all ingredients except for the cooking spray.
3. Add the toasted cumin and coriander seeds. Pulse until fine.
4. Shape the mixture into falafels and cover with cooking spray.
5. Preheat the air fryer to 390F and place falafels into the appliance.
6. Cook for 15 minutes or until the surface becomes golden brown.

Savory Air Fryer Potato Croquettes

- Ready in 25 minutes
- Servings: 10 croquettes

Ingredients

- ¼ cup nutritional yeast
- 2 cups boiled potatoes, mashed
- 1 flax mixture (1 tbsp flaxseed meal + 3 tbsp water)
- 2 tbsp flour
- 2 tbsp chives, chopped
- Salt and pepper to taste
- 2 tbsp vegetable oil
- ¼ cup bread crumbs

Directions

1. Preheat the air fryer to 400F.
2. In a large mixing bowl combine the nutritional yeast, potatoes, flax eggs, flour, and chives. Season with salt and pepper to taste and stir to combine well.
3. In another mixing bowl, combine the vegetable oil and bread crumbs until crumbly.
4. Form small balls of the potato mixture using your hands and dredge on the breadcrumb mixture.
5. Place to the air fryer basket and cook for 15 minutes or until the croquettes turn golden brown.

Unusual Kale and Potato Nuggets

- Ready in 35 minutes
- Servings: 2

Ingredients

- 1 tbsp olive oil
- 1 garlic clove, minced
- 2 cups kale, rinsed and chopped
- 1 cups boiled potatoes, finely chopped
- 1/8 cup milk
- ¼ tsp salt
- 1/8 tsp black pepper
- Cooking spray

Directions

1. Preheat the air fryer to 400F. Place a foil at the base of the air fryer basket and poke holes to allow air circulation.
2. Heat oil in a large skillet and sauté the garlic for 2 minutes. Add the kale until it wilts. Transfer to a large bowl.
3. Add the potatoes and pour in milk. Season with salt and pepper to taste, and stir to combine.
4. Form balls and spray with cooking oil.
5. Transfer to the air fryer basket and cook for 20 minutes or until golden brown.

Air Fried Zucchini Crisps

- Ready in 25 minutes
- Servings: 2

Ingredients

- ¼ cup breadcrumbs
- ¼ cup nutritional yeast
- ½ teaspoon garlic powder
- 1 green zucchini, sliced into thin rounds
- 1 tbsp olive oil

Directions

1. Place a foil at the base of the air fryer basket and poke holes. Preheat the air fryer to 400F.
2. In a large mixing bowl, combine the crumbs, nutritional yeast, and garlic powder.
3. In another bowl, toss sliced zucchini with the olive oil.
4. Dredge the zucchini slices with the crumb mixture and place inside the air fryer. Cook for 15 minutes or until crispy.
5. Serve with dipping sauce on your preference.

Air Fryer Snack and Appetizer Recipes

Mutton Chops

- Ready in 30 minutes
- Servings: 2

Ingredients

- 3 tablespoons vegetable oil
- 1 tablespoon of garam masala
- Salt and pepper, to taste
- 1 tablespoon of ginger
- 1 tablespoon of garlic powder
- 3 tablespoon of red chili pepper
- 2 large eggs
- 2 cups of breadcrumbs
- 1 pound mutton chops

Directions

1. Preheat the air fryer to 320F and sprinkle with oil.
2. In a large mixing bowl combine red chili pepper, garlic, ginger, pepper, salt and garam masala. Stir to combine.
3. Rub meat with these flavors.
4. In a shallow bowl beat eggs.
5. Take meat, place it in egg and after that in the cup of breadcrumbs.
6. Cook in the air fryer for 5-6 minutes. Flip the meat and cook for another 3-5 minutes.
7. Serve warm with salad or vegetables.

Easy and Quick Banana Chips

- Ready in 25 minutes
- Servings: 2

Ingredients

- 2 bananas
- ½ teaspoon of paprika
- ½ teaspoon of chat masala
- 3 tablespoons vegetable oil
- 2 cups of water

Directions

1. Peel bananas and cup them in the pieces.
2. In a large mixing bowl combine banana pieces with 1 tablespoon of oil, chat masala, pepper and paprika.
3. Preheat the air fryer to 280F.
4. Cook bananas for 10 minutes, shaking once while cooking.
5. Serve hot and surprise your guests.

Tortilla Chips

- Ready in 25 minutes
- Servings: 2

Ingredients

- 4 corn tortillas
- ½ teaspoon of salt
- ½ teaspoon of paprika
- ½ teaspoon of red chili pepper
- 3 tablespoons of oil

Directions

1. Sprinkle the frying basket with oil.
2. Preheat the Air Fryer to 280F.
3. Take tortillas and cut then in the slices, transfer to a bowl. Add salt, paprika and chili pepper there. Rub the pieces of tortillas with spices.
4. Then put them in the air fryer and cook for about 5-7 minutes. Shake well and cook for additional 3 minutes.
5. Serve hot with ketchup and enjoy with the scrumptious meal.

Delicious Potato Chips

- Ready in 30 minutes
- Servings: 2

Ingredients

- 3 large potatoes, sliced
- Salt and pepper, to taste½ teaspoon of salt
- ½ teaspoon of paprika
- ½ teaspoon of red chili pepper
- 2 tablespoons vegetable oil

Directions

1. Wash potatoes and slice them. Soak to the cold water for about 30 minutes.
2. Pat them dry, transfer to the large bowl and mix with salt, pepper, paprika, 1 tablespoon of oil and red chili pepper. Rub potatoes with the different spices.
3. Preheat the air fryer to 260F. Sprinkle the frying basket with oil, transfer potato slices and cook for about 15-20 minutes, shaking each 5 minutes, until cooked and crispy.
4. Serve and enjoy.

Grilled Broccoli

- Ready in 20 minutes
- Servings: 2

Ingredients

- 2 cups of broccoli
- 1 teaspoon of garlic powder
- 1 teaspoon of pepper
- ½ teaspoon of salt
- 1/8 teaspoon of paprika
- 1/6 teaspoon of oregano
- 1 tablespoon of olive oil
- 1 tablespoon of coconut oil
- 1 big red pepper
- ½ teaspoon of onion powder
- ½ cup of sauce

Directions

1. Wash and cup broccoli in the florets. Wash and chop the red pepper in the strings.
2. In a large mixing bowl combine the red pepper with broccoli.
3. Then add pepper, salt, paprika, oregano, coconut oil and onion powder to the bowl with vegetables. Stir to combine.
4. Preheat the air fryer to 350F.
5. Cook broccoli for 5 minutes. Then shake well, cover with sauce and cook for 5 minutes again.
6. Serve warm and you can decorate it with parsley or sprinkle with lemon.

Broccoli Pesto with Quinoa

- Ready in 30 minutes
- Servings: 2

Ingredients

- 1 cup of quinoa
- 2 cups of water
- 1 cup of broccoli
- 1 tablespoon of basil
- ½ teaspoon of salt
- ½ teaspoon of pepper
- ¼ cup of cream
- 2 tablespoons of lemon juice
- ¼ cup of oil
- 2/3 cup of almonds
- 4 garlic cloves
- 1/2 cup of cheese

Directions

1. Cook the quinoa with 2 cups of water. When it is ready, transfer it in the bowl.
2. Add broccoli and blend the products well. Season with salt, pepper, stir in chopped basil, almonds, cloves of garlic and blend the components well.
3. Preheat the air fryer to 350F and cook the mixture for about 10 minutes.
4. Then shake everything, add cream, lemon juice and cheese. Cook for 5 minutes more.
5. Enjoy with the meal.

Cauliflower Gratin

- Ready in 30 minutes
- Servings: 2

Ingredients

- 1 cauliflower head
- ¼ cup of cheese
- 1/8 teaspoon of ground nutmeg
- 1 cup of milk
- ½ teaspoon of salt
- ½ teaspoon of pepper
- 4 tablespoons of oil
- 2 tablespoons of flour

Directions

1. Preheat the air fryer to 350F.
2. Wash and clean cauliflower and cut it to the pieces.
3. Transfer to the air fryer.
4. In a large mixing bowl pour in the cup of milk, then season it with salt, pepper, flour, ground nutmeg there. Blend the components well. Pour the mixture to the air fryer.
5. Cook it for 15 minutes. Then cover with cheese and cook for 5 minutes more.
6. When ready serve and enjoy.

Mouth-Watering Side Air Fryer Recipes

Air Fryer Potato Chips

- Ready in 45 minutes
- Servings: 2

Ingredients

- 2 potatoes (russet or sweet)
- ½ tsp vegetable oil
- A pinch of salt to taste

Directions

1. Wash and slice the potatoes thin, round and neat. Soak the sliced potatoes in cold water for half an hour.
2. Blot dry and spread the sliced potatoes over shallow dish.
3. Mix salt and oil and pour it over the sliced potatoes.
4. Preheat the air fryer to 390F. Transfer potato slices and cook for 15 minutes, shaking couple times during cooking.
5. Serve the chips with ketchup or chili sauce and enjoy the right combination.

Flavorful Garlic Potatoes with Turkey

- Ready in 45 minutes
- Servings: 2

Ingredients

- 3 turkey strips (unsmoked) cooked
- 6 small potatoes
- 1 tsp garlic, minced
- 2 tsp olive oil
- Salt and black pepper, to taste

Directions

1. Peel and chop potatoes into fine cubes.
2. Preheat the air fryer to 350F. Sprinkle the cooking basket with the olive oil and cook potatoes for 10 minutes.
3. In a separate bowl cut turkey into fine pieces and mix with garlic, oil, salt and pepper. Add cooked potatoes into the bowl and mix well.
4. Put mixture on aluminum foil and cook for about 10 minutes.
5. Serve and enjoy.

Garlic Stuffed Mushrooms

- Ready in 25 minutes
- Servings: 2

Ingredients

- 6 mushrooms
- 1 small onion (peeled, diced)
- 1 tbsp breadcrumbs
- 1 tbsp olive oil
- 1 tsp garlic, minced
- 1 tsp parsley
- A pinch of salt and pepper

Directions

1. In a large mixing bowl, combine breadcrumbs, oil, onion, parsley, salt, pepper and garlic. Mix well.
2. Remove middle stalks from mushrooms and fill them with crumb mixture.
3. Preheat the air fryer to 350F. Cook mushrooms for about 10 minutes.

Roasted Potatoes and Yoghurt

- Ready in 50 minutes
- Servings: 2

Ingredients

- 1 pound potatoes
- 1 tbsp paprika
- Salt to taste
- Black pepper (freshly ground) to taste
- 1 tbsp olive oil
- 5.5 oz yoghurt (Greek)

Directions

1. Preheat the air fryer at 350F.
2. Peel and cut potatoes in small pieces of about 1-inch cubes, soak the pieces in cold water for 30 minutes. Then drain and pat dry the potato pieces.
3. In a medium size bowl add 1 tbsp. of oil, paprika and sprinkle pepper and stir well. Coat the cubes with the mixture.
4. Transfer to the air fryer and cook for about 20 minutes.
5. Serve them with yoghurt and enjoy.

Roasted Potatoes with Rosemary

- Ready in 30 minutes
- Servings: 2

Ingredients

- 2 large potatoes
- 1 tsp rosemary
- Salt and black pepper, to taste
- 1 tbsp olive oil

Directions

1. Peel potatoes and cut them into fine chunks for roasting.
2. Preheat the air fryer to 350F. Sprinkle the frying basket with the olive oil.
3. Cook potatoes for 10-15 minutes, shaking couple times during cooking.
4. Meanwhile, mix rosemary, salt and pepper in a bowl.
5. When potatoes ready, add to the bowl with rosemary mixture.
6. Serve as a side dish or as a separate dish. Enjoy.

Cheesy Rice Balls

- Ready in 40 minutes
- Servings: 2

Ingredients

- 1 cup rice, cooked
- 1 cup paneer
- 1 tbsp corn flour
- 1 green chili, chopped
- 1 cup cheese mozzarella, cubed
- 2 tbsp carrot, chopped
- 2 tbsp sweet corn
- 1 tbsp corn flour slurry
- Salt to taste
- Garlic powder to taste
- ½ cup breadcrumbs
- 1 tsp oregano

Directions

1. Preheat the air fryer to 390F.
2. In a large bowl combine all the ingredients. Mix well and form into small ball shape.
3. Roll the mixture in slurry and breadcrumbs. Cook for 15 minutes.
4. Serve and enjoy.

Classic French Fries

- Ready in 25 minutes
- Servings: 2

Ingredients

- 5 medium russet potatoes, peeled
- 2 tbsp olive oil
- Salt and black pepper, to taste

Directions

1. Peel the potatoes and cut them into 1/4 inch by 3 inch strips. Soak the potatoes in water for at least 30 minutes, then drain thoroughly and pat dry with a paper towel.
2. Preheat the Air Fryer to 360F.
3. Place the potatoes in a large bowl and sprinkle lightly with oil.
4. Transfer potatoes to the air fryer and cook for 15-20 minutes or until golden brown and crisp. Shake 2-3 times during cooking.

Delicious Grilled Cheese

- Ready in 25 minutes
- Servings: 2

Ingredients

- 4 slices of brioche or white bread
- ½ cup sharp cheddar cheese
- ¼ cup butter, melted

Directions

1. Preheat the air fryer to 360F. Place cheese and butter in separate bowls. Brush the butter on each side of the 4 slices of bread.
2. Place the cheese on 2 of the 4 pieces of bread.
3. Put the grilled cheese together and add to the cooking basket.
4. Cook for 5-7 minutes or until golden brown and the cheese has melted.

Roasted Brussels Sprouts

- Ready in 30 minutes
- Servings: 2

Ingredients

- 1 cups Brussels sprouts
- ¼ cup pine nuts (toasted)
- 1/2 orange (juice and zest)
- ¼ raisins, drained
- 1 tbsp olive oil olive

Directions

1. Preheat the air fryer to 390F.
2. Boil sprouts for about 4 minutes and then put them in cold water and drain the sprouts properly.
3. Meanwhile, soak raisins in orange juice for 15 minutes.
4. Now roast the cooled sprouts with oil for 15 minutes.
5. Serve with nuts, raisins and zest.

Turkey Wrapped Prawns

- Ready in 30 minutes
- Servings: 2

Ingredients

- 1 pound turkey, sliced
- 1 pound tiger prawns
- Salt and pepper to taste

Directions

1. Preheat the air fryer to 390F.
2. Wrap prawns with Turkey and secure with toothpick.
3. Refrigerate for 20 minutes.
4. Cook for 10 minutes in batches.
5. Serve with tartar sauce and enjoy the yummy taste.

Walnut Stilton Circles

- Ready in 40 minutes
- Servings: 2

Ingredients

- ¼ cup plain flour
- ¼ cup walnuts
- ¼ cup butter
- ¼ cup stilton

Directions

1. In a large mixing bowl combine all the ingredients, and mix them well till a thick texture appears. Cut dough into log shapes, approx. 1 inch.
2. Wrap it in aluminum foil and let it freeze for about 30 minutes.
3. Now cut the dough into circles.
4. Preheat the air fryer to 350F and line the basket with baking sheet.
5. Cook 20 minutes. And it is ready! Serve while hot.

Air Fryer Fish and Seafood Recipes

Crispy Air Fryer Catfish

- Ready in 30 minutes
- Servings: 2

Ingredients

- 2 fish fillets (catfish)
- 1 large egg
- 1 cup breadcrumbs
- 1 oz cup tortilla chips
- 1 lemon (juice and zest)
- 1 tsp parsley
- Salt and pepper, to taste

Directions

1. Cut fish fillets into neat pieces, then sprinkle them with lemon juice. Do not overdo it.
2. Combine breadcrumbs with lemon zest, parsley, tortillas, salt and pepper in a food processor. Lay the mixture in a tray spreading evenly.
3. Preheat the air fryer to 350F. Coat fish fillets with the mixture and cook for about 20-30 minutes, depending on fish size, until cooked.

Delicious Cajun Shrimp

- Ready in 25 minutes
- Servings: 2

Ingredients

- 1 pound shrimps
- ¼ tsp cayenne pepper
- ¼ tsp paprika (smoked)
- ½ tsp old bay seasoning
- 1 tbsp olive oil
- A pinch of salt

Directions

1. Preheat Air Fryer at 390F.
2. Mix all the ingredients mentioned in the ingredients list in a large bowl. Stir to combine well.
3. Coat the shrimps with the mixture.
4. Cook for 5 minutes.
5. Serve them with rice or any dipping sauce you prefer.

Air Fryer Crispy Crust Fish Fillets

- Ready in 25 minutes
- Servings: 2

Ingredients

- 2 fish fillets
- 1 egg, beaten
- 1 cup breadcrumbs
- 4 tbsp olive oil
- Black pepper and salt to taste

Directions

1. Preheat the Air Fryer to 350F.
2. In a shallow dish, combine together breadcrumbs, oil, pepper, and salt. In another dish add beaten egg.
3. Dip fish fillet in egg then coat with breadcrumbs and place in air fryer basket.
4. Cook fish fillets in the air fryer for 12 minutes.
5. Serve and enjoy.

Air Fried Salmon Croquettes

- Ready in 20 minutes
- Servings: 2

Ingredients

- 1/2 lb salmon fillet, chopped
- 2 egg whites
- 2 tbsp chives, chopped
- 2 tbsp garlic, minced
- ½ cup onion, chopped
- 2/3 cup carrots, grated
- 2/3 cup potato, grated
- ½ cup breadcrumbs
- ¼ cup plain flour
- Pepper and salt, to taste

Directions

1. Take three shallow dishes and in first dish add breadcrumbs with pepper and salt. Mix well.
2. In second dish add flour and in third dish add egg whites.
3. Now in mixing bowl add all remaining ingredients and mix well.
4. Make small balls from mixture and roll in flour then dip in egg and finally coat with breadcrumbs.
5. Preheat the air fryer to 320F. Place in air fryer basket and cook for 6 minutes.
6. Change temperature to 350F and cook for 4 minutes until crisp.
7. Serve hot and enjoy.

Easy Air Fryer Fish Strips

- Ready in 20 minutes
- Servings: 2

Ingredients

- 1 pound fish fillets on your preference, cut into strips
- ½ cup almond meal
- 1 tsp lemon pepper
- 1 egg white beaten
- Salt to taste

Directions

1. Preheat the air fryer to 400F.
2. In a shallow dish, combine together almond meal and lemon pepper.
3. In a small bowl add beaten egg white.
4. Dip fish strips in egg white then coat with almond meal and place in air fryer basket.
5. Cook for 12 minutes or until lightly golden brown.
6. Serve and enjoy.

Air Fried Cod Nuggets

- Ready in 30 minutes
- Servings: 2

Ingredients

- 1 pound cod fillet, cut into chunks
- 1 tbsp olive oil
- 1 cup cracker crumbs
- 1 tbsp egg and water
- cup plain flour
- Pepper and salt to taste

Directions

1. Add crackers crumb and oil in food processor and process until it forms into crumbs.
2. Season cod pieces with pepper and salt.
3. Coat seasoned cod pieces with flour then dip in egg and finally coated with cracker crumbs.
4. Preheat the Air Fryer to 350F. Cook fillets for about 15 minutes, turning once during cooking. Fry until lightly golden brown.
5. Serve hot and enjoy.

Crispy Air Fried Shrimp

- Ready in 20 minutes
- Servings: 2

Ingredients

- 1 pound shrimp, peeled and deveined
- 2 egg whites
- 2 tbsp olive oil
- 1/2 cup flour
- ½ tsp cayenne pepper
- 1 cup breadcrumbs
- Pepper and salt, to taste

Directions

1. In a shallow dish, combine together flour, pepper, and salt. In a small bowl add egg whites and whisk well.
2. In another shallow dish combine together breadcrumbs, cayenne pepper, and salt.
3. Preheat Air Fryer to 400F.
4. Coat shrimp with flour mixture then dip in egg white and finally coat with breadcrumbs.
5. Place coated shrimp in air fry basket and drizzle olive oil over them. Air fry shrimps for about 6-8 minutes.

Creamy Air Fryer Salmon

- Ready in 20 minutes
- Servings: 2

Ingredients

- 1 pound salmon, cut into 6 pieces
- ¼ cup yogurt
- 1 tbsp olive oil
- 1 tbsp dill, chopped
- 1 tbsp sour cream
- Salt to taste

Directions

1. Preheat the air fryer to 300F.
2. Season salmon with salt. Place salmon pieces in air fryer basket and drizzle with olive oil. Cook fish fillets for 10 minutes.
3. Meanwhile, combine together cream, dill, yogurt, and salt in a medium mixing bowl. Mix well.
4. Place salmon on serving dish and pour creamy sauce over salmon. Enjoy.

Air Fried Crab Herb Croquettes

- Ready in 30 minutes
- Servings: 2

Ingredients

- 1 pound crab meat
- 1 cup breadcrumbs
- 2 egg whites
- ½ tsp parsley
- ¼ tsp chives
- ¼ tsp tarragon
- 2 tbsp celery, chopped
- ¼ cup red pepper, chopped
- 1 tsp olive oil
- 1 tsp lime juice
- 4 tbsp sour cream
- 4 tbsp mayonnaise
- ¼ cup onion, chopped
- ¼ tsp salt

Directions

1. Place breadcrumbs and salt in a bowl. Stir to combine.
2. In a small bowl, add egg whites.
3. Add all remaining ingredients into the 3rd bowl and mix well to combine.
4. Preheat the air fryer to 330F.
5. Make croquettes from the mixture and dip in egg white and coat with breadcrumbs. Place to the air fryer basket and cook for about 15-20 minutes, until ready and crispy.
6. Serve and enjoy.

Super Cheesy Breaded Salmon

- Ready in 30 minutes
- Servings: 2

Ingredients

- 2 cups breadcrumbs
- 2 filets of salmon
- 1 cup Swiss cheese, shredded
- 2 eggs, beaten

Directions

1. Preheat your air fryer to 390F.
2. Dip each salmon filet into the egg mixture, then top with Swiss cheese.
3. Dip into the breadcrumbs and coat all sides of the fish.
4. Place on an oven safe dish and cook for 20 minutes.
5. Serve and enjoy.

Parmesan-Crusted Tilapia

- Ready in 20 minutes
- Servings: 2

Ingredients

- 2 tilapia fillets
- ¾ cup grated parmesan cheese
- 1 tbsp olive oil
- 1 tbsp chopped parsley
- 2 tsp paprika
- Pinch of garlic powder
- Pinch of salt and black pepper, to taste

Directions

1. Preheat your air fryer to 350F. Sprinkle the olive oil over the tilapia fillets.
2. Combine all of the remaining ingredients in a shallow bowl. Coat the tilapia fillets with the parmesan mixture.
3. Line a baking dish with parchment paper and arrange the fillets on it.
4. Place in the air fryer and cook for 5 minutes.
5. Serve and enjoy.

Air Fryer Poultry Recipes

Chicken Nuggets

- Ready in 35 minutes
- Servings: 2

Ingredients

- 1 pound chicken breast, chopped
- 1 cup breadcrumbs
- 1 garlic clove, minced
- 1 tsp tomato ketchup
- 2 large eggs
- 1 tbsp vegetable oil
- 1 tsp paprika
- 1 tsp parsley
- Salt and pepper to taste

Directions

1. Make a batter using breadcrumbs, paprika, salt, pepper and oil. Mix the ingredients well to make a thick paste.
2. In a large bowl combine chopped chicken, parsley, one egg and ketchup.
3. Make the chicken mixture into a nugget shape and dip it in other egg, then add in crumbs for coating.
4. Preheat the air fryer to 380 F. Cook nuggets for about 20 minutes, turning once, until both sides are crisp.
5. Serve it with mayo dip to enjoy the combined flavor.

Crispy Chicken Drumsticks

- Ready in 35 minutes
- Servings: 2

Ingredients

- 4 chicken drumsticks
- 1 tsp cayenne pepper
- 2 tbsp mustard powder
- 2 tbsp oregano
- 2 tbsp thyme
- 3 tbsp coconut milk
- 1 large egg, beaten
- 1/3 cup cauliflower
- 1/3 cup oats
- Pepper and salt to taste

Directions

1. Preheat the air fryer to 350F.
2. Season chicken drumsticks with pepper and salt. Rub coconut milk all over chicken drumsticks.
3. Add all ingredients except egg into the food processor and process until it looks like breadcrumbs.
4. Transfer food processor mixture into the bowl. In another small bowl beaten egg.
5. Dip each chicken drumstick in breadcrumb mixture then dip in egg and again dip in breadcrumbs.
6. Place coated chicken drumsticks in air fryer basket and cook for 20 minutes.
7. Serve hot and enjoy.

Flavorful Curry Chicken

- Ready in 50 minutes
- Servings: 2

Ingredients

- 2 chicken thighs
- 1 zucchini (small)
- 2 garlic cloves
- 6 apricots (dried)
- 3.5 oz turnip (long)
- 6 basil leaves
- 1 tbsp pistachios (whole)
- 1 tbsp raisin soup
- 1 tbsp oil (olive)
- 1 large pinch salt
- 1 pinch pepper
- 1 tsp curry powder

Directions

1. Preheat the air fryer at 320F.
2. Cut the chicken into 2 fine pieces. Cut vegetables into bite sizes.
3. Add all ingredients in a dish and stir to combine well.
4. Transfer the chicken with vegetables to the air fryer basket and cook for about 30 minutes, shaking couple times. Cook until crisp and ready.
5. Serve.

Garlic Lemon Chicken

- Ready in 25 minutes
- Servings: 2

Ingredients

- 1 pound chicken breast
- 1 tsp garlic, minced
- 1 tbsp chicken seasoning
- 1 lemon juice
- Handful black peppercorns
- Pepper and salt to taste

Directions

1. Preheat the air fryer to 350F.
2. Season chicken with pepper and salt. Rub chicken seasoning all over chicken breast and place seasoned chicken on aluminum foil sheet. Add garlic, lemon juice, and black peppercorns over chicken and seal foil tightly.
3. Place chicken in the air fryer basket and cook for 15 minutes.
4. Open foil and serve.

Delicious Bacon Wrapped Chicken

- Ready in 25 minutes
- Servings: 2

Ingredients

- 1 pound chicken breast, cut into 6 pieces
- 6 rashers back bacon
- 1 tbsp soft cheese
- Salt and pepper, to taste

Directions

1. Place bacon rashers on dish and spread soft cheese over them.
2. Place chicken pieces on each bacon rashers and roll up them and secure with wooden stick.
3. Preheat the air fryer to 350F. Place chicken rolls in air fryer basket and cook for 15 minutes, until done.
4. Serve and enjoy.

Spicy Chicken Wings

- Ready in 20 minutes
- Servings: 2

Ingredients

- 6 chicken wings
- 1 tbsp honey
- 2 garlic cloves, chopped
- 1 tsp red chili flakes
- 2 tbsp Worcestershire sauce
- Pepper and salt to taste

Directions

1. Add all ingredients except chicken wings in bowl and mix well. Then, add chicken wings and mix well and place in refrigerator for 1 hour.
2. Preheat the air fryer to 320F. Place marinated chicken wings into the air fryer basket and cook for about 10 minutes.
3. Increase heat to 370 F and cook for another 4-6 minutes, until crisp.
4. Serve hot and enjoy.

Roasted Whole Chicken with Herbs

- Ready in 1 hour
- Servings: 1 whole chicken

Ingredients

- 5-7 pounds whole chicken with skin
- 3 garlic cloves, minced
- 1 tbsp onion powder
- 1 tsp dried thyme
- 1 tsp dried basil
- 1 tsp dried rosemary
- ½ tsp black pepper
- 2 tsp salt
- 2 tbsp extra virgin olive oil

Directions

1. Rub the chicken with salt, pepper, herbs, and olive oil. Set aside for at least 20-30 minutes.
2. Meanwhile, preheat the Air Fryer to 340 F.
3. Cook chicken for 18-20 minutes, and then carefully turn for another side. Cook for another 20 minutes, until ready.
4. When cooked, let the chicken rest for 10 minutes, then slice and serve.

Herb Orange Chicken Wings

- Ready in 40-50 minutes
- Servings: 2

Ingredients

- 6 chicken wings
- 1 tbsp Worcestershire sauce
- 1 tbsp sugar
- 1 orange juice and zest
- ½ tsp thyme, dried
- ½ tsp sage
- 1 tsp mint
- 1 tsp basil
- ½ tsp oregano
- 1 tsp parsley
- 1 tsp rosemary
- A pinch of salt and pepper to taste

Directions

1. Add chicken and all remaining ingredients into the mixing bowl and mix well. Transfer chicken into the refrigerator for 30 minutes.
2. Meanwhile, preheat the air fryer to 350F.
3. Wrap marinated chicken in aluminum foil with juices. Cook in the air fryer for about 20-30 minutes.
4. Open foil wrap chicken and discard orange zest and air fry chicken wings at 350F for another 15 minutes.
5. Serve hot and enjoy.

Buffalo Wings

- Ready in 40 minutes
- Servings: 2

Ingredients

- 1 pound chicken wings, without the wing tips
- ¼ cup + ¼ cup hot sauce, separately
- 3 + 3 tbsp melted butter, separately
- Sea salt to taste
- Blue cheese, optional
- Celery sticks, optional

Directions

1. Prepare the chicken wings: divide the drumettes from the wingettes. Place them into the bowl.
2. In another bowl mix together 3 tablespoons of melted butter and ¼ cup of hot sauce stirring them well.
3. Cover the chicken pieces with this mixture and marinate it for 2 hours or even overnight.
4. Preheat the air fryer to 400F. Place wings into the air fryer and cook for about 12 minutes, shaking halfway.
5. Meanwhile, prepare the sauce: mix the remaining 3 table-spoons of butter and the remaining ¼ cup of hot sauce.
6. Dip the cooked wings in this sauce and serve. It tastes great with the blue cheese and celery sticks.

Easy Teriyaki Chicken

- Ready in 30 minutes
- Servings: 2

Ingredients

- 2 chicken drumsticks, boneless
- 1 tsp ginger, grated
- 1 tbsp cooking wine
- 3 tbsp teriyaki sauce

Directions

1. Add all ingredients into the bowl and mix well and place in refrigerator for 30 minutes.
2. Preheat the air fryer to 350F. Add marinated chicken in Air Fryer baking pan and cook for 10 minutes. Then flip the chicken to other side and Cook at 380F for 6 minutes. Serve hot and enjoy.

Air Fryer Pork and Lamb Recipes

Sweet and Sour Delicious Pork

- Ready in 35 minutes
- Servings: 2

Ingredients

- 1 pound pork tenderloin, trimmed of fat, cut into strips
- 1 tablespoon corn flour (+ extra for coating)
- 4 fl oz red wine
- 10 fl oz tomato sauce or passata
- 1 tablespoon tomato paste or tomato puree
- 5 fl oz unsweetened apple juice
- 1 tablespoon brown sugar
- 2 sliced onions
- 2 cloves finely chopped garlic
- 2 tablespoons red wine vinegar
- 2 tablespoons olive oil
- Salt and freshly ground pepper to taste

Directions

1. Mix in a large bowl corn flour with red wine until smooth than add there tomato sauce, apple juice, vinegar, sugar, tomato paste, season and mix thoroughly. Set bowl aside.
2. Coat chopped meat in corn flour and set aside.
3. Preheat the air fryer to 350F.
4. Slice onions and put them into air fryer. Pour the olive oil over them. Cook for 5 minutes.
5. Add coated with flour pork and finely chopped garlic. Cook for another 5 minutes.

6. Stir the pork to separate the pieces and add them to the sweet and sour sauce. Cook for 10 minutes or until the pork tender and the sauce thick.
7. Season to taste.

Char Siu

- Ready in 25 minutes
- Servings: 2

Ingredients

- 1 pound pork
- 3 tablespoon hoisin sauce
- 3 tablespoon sugar
- 3 tablespoon soy sauce
- 2 tablespoon corn syrup
- 2 tablespoon mirin
- 2 tablespoon olive oil
- Salt and pepper to taste

Directions

1. Cut pork into 2-inch stripes.
2. Mix all ingredients besides oil together in a large bowl, and then put the meat into marinade. Set aside at least for 40 minutes.
3. Discard marinade and sprinkle pork with olive oil.
4. Preheat the air fryer to 380F. Cook the meat for 15 minutes, turning once during cooking.
5. Serve.

Country Fried Steak

- Ready in 30 minutes
- Servings: 2

Ingredients

- 2 pieces 6-ounce sirloin steak pounded thin
- 2 eggs, beaten
- 1 ½ cup all-purpose flour
- 1 ½ cup breadcrumbs
- 1 teaspoon onion powder
- 1 teaspoon garlic powder
- Salt and pepper, to taste

Directions

1. Combine the breadcrumbs, onion, and garlic powder, salt and pepper in a large mixing bowl. Mix well.
2. In other bowls place flour and beat eggs.
3. Dip the steak in this order: flour, eggs, and seasoned breadcrumbs.
4. Preheat the air fryer to 380F.
5. Cook breaded steak for 6-7 minutes, turn over once and cook for another 5-7 minutes until becomes golden and crispy.
6. Serve and enjoy.

Easy Cooking Pork Chop

- Ready in 35 minutes
- Servings: 2

Ingredients

- 2 middle pieces pork chop
- 1 tablespoon plain flour
- 1 egg, beaten
- 2 tablespoon olive oil
- 3 tablespoon breadcrumbs
- Salt and ground pepper for seasoning

Directions

1. Season pork chop with salt and ground pepper from both sides.
2. In three different bowls place plain flour, beaten egg, and breadcrumbs.
3. Coat each pork chop from both sides first with flour then with egg and with breadcrumbs.
4. Preheat the air fryer to 380°F
5. Place coated pork chops into the Fryer and cook for 10 minutes from one side and 5 minutes from another side.
6. Serve with cooked rice and mashed potatoes.

Pork Satay with Peanut Sauce

- Ready in 30 minutes
- Servings: 2

Ingredients

- 1 pound pork chops, cut into 1-inch cubes
- 2 garlic, minced
- 1 tablespoon fresh ginger, grated
- 2 teaspoons chili paste
- 2-3 tablespoons sweet soy sauce
- 2 tablespoons vegetable oil
- 1 shallot, finely chopped
- 1 teaspoon ground coriander
- ½ cup coconut milk
- 4 oz unsalted butter

Directions

1. Mix half of the garlic in a dish with the ginger, 1 teaspoon hot pepper sauce, 1 tablespoon soy sauce, and 1 tablespoon oil. Add the the meat to the mixture and leave to marinate for 15 minutes.
2. Preheat the air fryer to 380 F. Put the marinated meat in the air fryer basket cook for 12 minutes until brown and done. Turn once while cooking.
3. Meanwhile, make the peanut sauce. Heat 1 tablespoon of the oil in a saucepan and gently sauté the shallot with garlic. Add the coriander and cook for 1-2 minutes more. Mix the coconut milk and the peanuts with 1 teaspoon hot pepper sauce and 1 tablespoon soy sauce with the shallot mixture and gently boil for 5 minutes, stirring constantly.
4. Serve the meat with sauce and enjoy!

Zero Oil Pork Chops

- Ready in 25 minutes
- Servings: 2

Ingredients

- 2 pieces pork chops
- 1 tablespoon of plain flour
- 1 large egg
- 2 tablespoon breadcrumbs
- Salt and black pepper to taste

Directions

1. Preheat the air fryer to 360 F.
2. Season pork chops with salt and black pepper and set aside.
3. Beat the egg in the plate. In another plate place the flour and in the third plate - breadcrumbs.
4. Cover each pork chop with the flour on both sides, then, dip in the egg, then, cover with breadcrumbs. Make sure that meat covered from all sides.
5. Place pork chops in the air fryer and cook for 15 minutes, until they are tender and crispy. Turn once while cooking, to cook the meat from both sides.
6. Serve with fresh vegetables or mashed potatoes.

Delicious Pork Tenderloin

- Ready in 35 minutes
- Servings: 2

Ingredients

- 1 pound pork tenderloin
- 1 medium red or yellow pepper, sliced
- 1 large red onion, sliced
- 2 tablespoon Provencal herbs
- 1 tablespoon Olive oil
- ½ tablespoon mustard
- Ground black pepper
- Salt, to taste

Directions

1. In the large bowl mix sliced pepper and onion, Provencal herbs, salt and ground pepper to taste. Also, add olive oil to this mixture.
2. Cut the pork tenderloin into 4-6 large pieces, scrub with salt, ground pepper, and mustard.
3. Preheat your Air Fryer to 370-390° F.
4. Place vegetable mixture to the air fryer.
5. Coat meat pieces with olive oil and place them up to the vegetables.
6. Cook for 15 minutes until meat and vegetables will become roasted.
7. Turn the meat and vegetable in the middle of cooking process.

Drunken Ham with Mustard

- Ready in 50 minutes
- Servings: 2

Ingredients

- 1 joint of ham, approximately 1-2 pounds
- 2 tablespoon honey
- 2 tablespoon French mustard
- 8 oz whiskey
- 1 teaspoon Provencal herbs
- 1 tablespoon salt

Directions

1. In a large casserole dish that fits in your air fryer prepare the marinade: combine the whiskey, honey and mustard. Mix well.
2. Place the ham in the oven dish and turn it in the marinade.
3. Preheat the Air Fryer to 380 F and cook the ham for 15 minutes.
4. Add another shot of whiskey and turn in the marinade again. Cook the ham for 25 minutes until done.
5. Serve with potatoes and fresh vegetables.

Spicy Lamb Chops

- Ready nearly in 1 hour
- Servings: 2

Ingredients

- 2 lamb chops
- 1 teaspoon cumin
- ½ teaspoon chili powder
- 2 tablespoons lime juice
- 4 tablespoons low-fat yogurt
- 1 tablespoon crushed coriander seeds
- 2 teaspoons garam masala
- 1 teaspoon salt

Directions

1. In a large mixing bowl combine lime juice, yogurt, salt, and spices. Mix well. Use the mixture to make a coating for the lamb chops. Set aside for about an hour.
2. Meanwhile, preheat the air fryer to 380 F. Place the chops and cook them for approximately 15 minutes.
3. Serve.

Grilled Vegetables with Lamb

- Ready in 30 minutes
- Servings: 2

Ingredients

- 2 lamb chops
- ½ bunch fresh mint
- 4 tablespoons olive oil
- 1 small parsnip
- 1 large carrot
- 1 fennel bulb
- Salt and pepper, to taste
- Fresh rosemary

Directions

1. Chop the mint and rosemary. Add 4 tablespoons of olive oil and season the marinade with salt and pepper. Marinate the lamb chops for at least 3 hours.
2. Cut the vegetables into small cubes and leave them to soak in a container of water.
3. Preheat the air fryer to 380 F and sear the lamb chops for 2 minutes. Remove the chops from the basket and cover the bottom with vegetables. Place the lamb chops on top.
4. Cook for another 6 minutes and then serve hot.

Carrot Lamb Meatballs

- Ready in 25 minutes
- Servings: 2

Ingredients

- 1 pound ground lamb
- 3 medium carrots, grated
- 3 large eggs, beaten
- 2 garlic cloves, minced
- ½ teaspoon ground pepper
- ½ teaspoon salt

Directions

1. Preheat the air fryer to 380 F.
2. Mix all ingredients in the large mixing bowl. Form medium-sized meatballs with hands.
3. Place them in the air fryer and cook for 15 minutes, until ready and crispy.
4. Serve with vegetables or steamed rice.

Lamb Chops with Garlic Sauce

- Ready in 45 minutes
- Servings: 2

Ingredients

- 2 lamb chops
- 2 garlic cloves
- 3 tablespoons olive oil
- 1 tablespoon fresh oregano, chopped
- Salt freshly ground black pepper, to taste

Directions

1. Preheat the air fryer 390 F.
2. Add 1/2 of the olive oil in the air fryer basket and place garlic cloves. Close and cook for 3-5 minutes until golden and fragrant.
3. Meanwhile, mix olive oil with herbs with some salt and pepper. Coat lamb chops with oil mixture and place to the fryer. Cook for about 20 minutes until ready.
4. Serve and enjoy.

Delicious Lamb Patties

- Ready in 30 minutes
- Servings: 2

Ingredients

- 1 pound ground lamb meat
- 2 large eggs, beaten
- ½ teaspoon ground caraway
- ½ teaspoon ground basil
- 1 teaspoon garlic salt

Directions

1. Combine all ingredients in a large mixing bowl. Stir to combine well.
2. Preheat the air fryer to 370 F.
3. Form medium-sized patties from the meat mixture and place them to the air fryer. Cook for about 15-18 minutes, until cooked and browned.
4. Serve and enjoy!

Air Fryer Beef Recipes

Simple Air Fried Beef Steak

- Ready in 20 minutes
- Servings: 2

Ingredients

- 2 pcs 2-inch thick beef steak
- Pepper and salt to taste
- 1 tsp butter for serving

Directions

1. Preheat the Air Fryer 400F.
2. Add beef steak in Air Fryer baking tray and season with pepper and salt.
3. Cook beef steak in preheated Air Fryer for 3 minutes.
4. Flip steak to other side and cook for another 3 minutes. Serve with a teaspoon butter and enjoy.

Crispy Crust Beef Schnitzel

- Ready in 25 minutes
- Servings: 2

Ingredients

- 2 thin beef schnitzel
- 1 egg, beaten
- ½ cup breadcrumbs
- 2 tbsp olive oil
- Pepper and salt to taste

Directions

1. Preheat the air fryer to 350F.
2. In a shallow dish, combine together breadcrumbs, oil, pepper, and salt. In another shallow dish add beaten egg.
3. Dip schnitzel into the egg then coat with breadcrumbs.
4. Place coated schnitzel in air fryer basket and air fry for 12 minutes.
5. Serve and enjoy.

Amazingly Easy Air Fryer Meatloaf

- Ready in 30 minutes
- Servings: 1 meatloaf

Ingredients

- 1 pound ground beef
- 1 egg, beaten
- 1 tbsp thyme
- 1 small onion, chopped
- 3 tbsp breadcrumbs
- Salt and pepper to taste

Directions

1. Preheat the Air Fryer 400F.
2. Add all ingredients into the mixing bowl and mix well until combined.
3. Add meatloaf mixture into the loaf pan and place in Air Fryer basket.
4. Cook in preheated Air Fryer for 25 minutes.
5. Cut into slices and serve.

Stuffed Bell Pepper

- Ready in 30 minutes
- Servings: 2

Ingredients

- 2 bell peppers, cut top of bell pepper
- 1/2 cup ground beef
- 2/3 cup cheese, shredded
- ½ cup rice, cooked
- 1 tsp basil, dried
- ½ tsp chili powder
- 1/2 tsp black pepper
- 1 tsp garlic salt
- 2 tsp Worcestershire sauce
- 8 oz tomato sauce
- 2 garlic cloves, minced
- 1 small onion, chopped

Directions

1. Spray pan with cooking spray and sauté onion and garlic in pan over medium heat. Add beef, basil, chili powder, black pepper, and garlic salt. Mix well and cook until meat brown. Remove pan from heat.
2. Add half cheese, rice, Worcestershire sauce, and tomato sauce in pan and mix well to combine.
3. Stuff beef mixture into bell peppers equally.
4. Preheat the Air Fryer 400F. Spray Air Fryer basket with cooking spray.
5. Place stuffed bell peppers in Air Fryer basket and cook for 11 minutes.
6. Once timer is off then top bell pepper with remaining cheese and cook for another 2 minutes until cheese is melted.
7. Serve and enjoy.

Marinated Beef and Broccoli

- Ready in 25 minutes
- Servings: 2

Ingredients

- 1/2 cup broccoli, cut into florets
- 1/2 pound round steak, cut into strips
- 1 garlic clove, minced
- 1 tsp ginger, minced
- 1 tbsp olive oil
- 1 tsp cornstarch
- 1 tsp sugar
- 1 tsp soy sauce
- 1/3 cup sherry wine
- 2 tsp sesame oil
- 1/3 cup oyster sauce

Directions

1. Add sugar, soy sauce, sherry wine, cornstarch, sesame oil, and oyster sauce in a bowl and mix well.
2. Add steak strips into the bowl mix well and set aside for 45 minutes.
3. Preheat the air fryer to 350F.
4. Add broccoli in air fryer then add marinated steak on top.
5. Sprinkle with the olive oil, garlic and ginger over broccoli and steak mixture.
6. Cook at 350F for 12 minutes.
7. Serve hot with rice and enjoy.

Delicious Cheesy Burger Patties

- Ready in 20 minutes
- Servings: 2

Ingredients

- 1 pound ground beef
- 2 cheddar cheese slices
- Pepper and salt to taste

Directions

1. Preheat the air fryer to 350F.
2. Season ground beef with pepper and salt.
3. Make two equal patties from mixture and place in air fryer basket.
4. Fry patties for 10 minutes. After 10 minutes place cheese slices over patties and air fry for another 1 minute.
5. Serve with buns and enjoy.

Sweet and Tangy Meatballs

- Ready in 30 minutes
- Servings: nearly 20+ meatballs

Ingredients

- 1 pound beef mince
- 1 tbsp lemon juice
- ¼ cup vinegar
- 1 tbsp Worcestershire sauce
- tbsp Tabasco
- ¾ cup tomato ketchup
- 3 gingersnaps cookies, crushed
- ½ tsp dry mustard
- ½ cup brown sugar

Directions

1. In a large mixing bowl combine all the ingredients and mix well.
2. Preheat the air fryer to 370F.
3. Roll small meatballs with hands and place them to the air fryer basket.
4. Cook for about 15 minutes, then serve and enjoy.

Air Fried Roast Beef

- Ready in 1 hour
- Servings: 2

Ingredients

- 1 pound beef
- 1 tbsp olive oil
- 1 tsp dried rosemary
- 1 tsp dried thyme
- ½ tsp black pepper
- ½ tsp oregano
- ½ tsp of garlic powder
- A pinch of salt
- 1 tsp onion powder

Directions

1. Preheat the air fryer to 330F.
2. In a small bowl combine all spices.
3. Brush the olive oil over the beef. Rub the spice mixture into the meat.
4. Place meat in the air fryer and cook for 30 minutes.
5. Flip it over and cook for 25 more minutes.
6. Serve and enjoy.

Crispy Beef Cubes

- Ready in 30 minutes
- Servings: 2

Ingredients

- 1 pound beef loin
- 1 jar (16 oz) cheese pasta sauce
- 1/2 cup breadcrumbs
- Salt and black pepper, to taste
- 1 tbsp extra virgin olive oil

Directions

1. Cut beef into 1-inch cubes and transfer to a mixing bowl and coat with pasta sauce.
2. In another bowl combine breadcrumbs, olive oil, salt and pepper. Stir to combine.
3. Place beef cubes to a breadcrumb mixture and coat from all sides.
4. Preheat the air fryer to 380F. Cook beef cubes for 12-15 minutes, stirring occasionally, until ready and crispy.
5. Serve hot and enjoy.

Beef Steak

- Ready in 15 minutes
- Servings: 2

Ingredients

- 2 steaks, thickness of 1 inch
- 1 tbsp olive oil
- Black pepper and salt, to taste

Directions

1. Preheat the air fryer with the baking tray inside for 390F.
2. Sprinkle both sides of the steak with the oil. Sprinkle both sides with salt and pepper.
3. Carefully lay the steak on the preheated baking tray.
4. Cook for 3 minutes in the air fryer. Then turn the steak around and cook for another 3 minutes.
5. When ready, remove and set aside for about 3 minutes and serve.

Air Fryer Vegetable Recipes

Balsamic Artichokes

- Ready in 20 minutes
- Servings: 2

Ingredients

- 2 big artichokes, trimmed
- Salt and black pepper to taste
- 2 tablespoons lemon juice
- ¼ cup extra virgin olive oil
- 2 teaspoons balsamic vinegar
- 1 teaspoon oregano, dried
- 2 garlic cloves, minced

Directions

1. Preheat the air fryer to 360F.
2. Season artichokes with salt and pepper, rub them with half of the oil and half of the lemon juice, put them in your air fryer and cook for 7 minutes.
3. Meanwhile, in a medium bowl mix the rest of the lemon juice with vinegar, the remaining oil, salt, pepper, garlic and oregano and stir very well.
4. Arrange artichokes on a platter, drizzle the balsamic vinaigrette mixture over them and serve.

Beet Salad and Parsley Dressing

- Ready in 25 minutes
- Servings: 2

Ingredients

- 2 large beets
- 2 tbsp balsamic vinegar
- A bunch of parsley, chopped
- Salt and black pepper to taste
- 1 tablespoon extra virgin olive oil
- 1 garlic clove, chopped
- 2 tablespoons capers

Directions

1. Preheat the air fryer to 360F. Put beets in your air fryer and cook them for 14 minutes.
2. Meanwhile, in a bowl, mix parsley with garlic, salt, pepper, olive oil and capers and stir very well.
3. Transfer beets to a cutting board, leave them to cool down, peel them, slice and put in a salad bowl.
4. Add vinegar, drizzle the parsley dressing all over and serve.

Beets and Blue Cheese Salad

- Ready in 25 minutes
- Servings: 2

Ingredients

- 2 beets, peeled and quartered
- Salt and black pepper to the taste
- ¼ cup blue cheese, crumbled
- 1 tablespoon olive oil

Directions

1. Preheat the air fryer to 350F.
2. Place beets in your air fryer and cook them for 14 minutes and transfer them to a bowl.
3. Add blue cheese, salt, pepper and oil, toss and serve.

Beet, Tomato and Goat Cheese Mix

- Ready in 35 minutes
- Servings: 2

Ingredients

- 1 small beet, trimmed, peeled and halved
- 1 small red onion, sliced
- 4 ounces goat cheese, crumbled
- 1 tablespoon balsamic vinegar
- Salt and black pepper to taste
- 1 tbsp sugar
- 1 pint mixed cherry tomatoes, halved
- 2 ounces pecans
- 2 tablespoons olive oil

Directions

1. Preheat the air fryer to 340F.
2. Transfer beet in your air fryer, season them with salt and pepper, cook for 14 minutes and transfer to a salad bowl.
3. Add onion, cherry tomatoes and pecans and toss.
4. In another bowl, mix vinegar with sugar and oil, whisk well until sugar dissolves and add to salad.
5. Also add goat cheese, toss and serve.

Broccoli Salad

- Ready in 30 minutes
- Servings: 2

Ingredients

- 1 medium-sized broccoli head, florets separated
- 1 tablespoon peanut oil
- 2 garlic cloves, minced
- 1 tablespoon Chinese rice wine vinegar
- Salt and black pepper to taste

Directions

1. In a large bowl mix broccoli with salt, pepper and half of the oil. Stir to combine well.
2. Preheat the air fryer to 350F. Transfer the broccoli mixture to the air fryer basket and cook for about 8 minutes, shaking the fryer halfway.
3. Transfer broccoli to a salad bowl, add the rest of the peanut oil, garlic and rice vinegar, toss really well and serve.

Brussels Sprouts and Tomatoes Mix

- Ready in 20 minutes
- Servings: 2

Ingredients

- 1 pound Brussels sprouts, trimmed
- Salt and black pepper to taste
- 4 cherry tomatoes, halved
- ¼ cup green onions, chopped1 tablespoon olive oil

Directions

1. Preheat the air fryer to 350F.
2. Season Brussels sprouts with salt and pepper, put them in your air fryer and cook for 10 minutes.
3. Transfer them to a bowl, add salt, pepper, cherry tomatoes, green onions and olive oil, toss well and serve.

Spicy Fried Cabbage

- Ready in 20 minutes
- Servings: 2

Ingredients

- 1 small cabbage, cut into 8 wedges
- 1 tablespoon sesame seed oil
- 1 carrots, grated
- ¼ cup apple cider vinegar
- ¼ cups apple juice
- ½ teaspoon cayenne pepper
- ½ teaspoon red pepper flakes, crushed

Directions

1. In a pan that fits your air fryer, combine cabbage with oil, carrot, vinegar, apple juice, cayenne and pepper flakes. Toss to combine.
2. Preheat the air fryer to 350F and place the pan into the fryer. Cook for about 8 minutes.
3. When ready, divide cabbage mix on plates and serve.

Sweet Baby Carrots

- Ready in 20 minutes
- Servings: 2

Ingredients

- 1 cup baby carrots
- A pinch of salt and black pepper
- 2 tsp brown sugar
- 1 ½ tablespoon butter, melted

Directions

1. In a dish that fits your air fryer, mix baby carrots with butter, salt, pepper and sugar. Stir to combine well.
2. Preheat the air fryer to 340F. Place the cooking dish to the air fryer and cook for about 10-12 minutes, until tender and cooked.
3. Divide among plates and serve.

Herbed Eggplant and Zucchini Mix

- Ready in 15 minutes
- Servings: 2

Ingredients

- 1 medium-sized eggplant, roughly cubed
- 1 zucchinis, roughly cubed
- 1 tablespoons lemon juice
- Salt and black pepper to taste
- 1 teaspoon thyme, dried
- 1 teaspoon oregano, dried
- 3 tablespoons olive oil

Directions

1. In a large mixing bowl combine the eggplant, zucchinis, lemon juice, salt, pepper, thyme, oregano and olive oil. Stir to combine well.
2. Preheat the air fryer to 360F.
3. Transfer vegetable mixture to the dish that fits your air fryer basket, then put the dish to the fryer. Cook for about 10-15 minutes, until cooked and tender.
4. Divide among plates and serve right away.

Flavored Fennel

- Ready in 20 minutes
- Servings: 2

Ingredients

- 1 fennel bulb, cut into quarters
- 3 tablespoons olive oil
- Salt and black pepper to taste
- 1 garlic clove, minced
- 1 red chili pepper, chopped
- ¾ cup veggie stock
- Juice from ½ lemon
- ¼ cup white wine
- ¼ cup parmesan, grated

Directions

1. Heat up a pan that fits your air fryer with the oil over medium high heat, add garlic and chili pepper, stir and cook for 2 minutes.
2. Add fennel, salt, pepper, stock, wine, lemon juice, and parmesan, toss to coat.
3. Preheat the air fryer to 350F. Transfer all the vegetables to the air fryer basket and cook for about 6-10 minutes.
4. When cooked, serve to the plates and enjoy.

Air Fryer Dessert Recipes

Easy Pineapple Sticks

- Ready in 20 minutes
- Servings: 2

Ingredients

- ½ fresh pineapple, cut into sticks
- ¼ cup desiccated coconut

Directions

1. Preheat the air fryer to 400F.
2. Roll pineapple sticks into the desiccated coconut and place in air fryer basket. Cook for about 10 minutes
3. Serve and enjoy.

Banana Oats Cookies

- Ready in 20 minutes
- Servings: 20+ cookies

Ingredients

- 2 cups quick oats
- ¼ cup milk
- 3 ripe bananas, mashed
- ¼ cup coconut shredded

Directions

1. Preheat the Air Fryer to 350F.
2. Add all ingredients into the bowl and mix well to combine.
3. Spoon cookie dough onto baking sheet and place in air fryer basket.
4. Bake cookies for 15 minutes, until cooked
5. Serve and enjoy.

Crisp and Sweet Bananas

- Ready in 20 minutes
- Servings: 2

Ingredients

- 2 ripe bananas
- 1 tbsp almond meal
- 1 tbsp cashew, crush
- 1 egg, beaten
- 1 ½ tbsp coconut Oil
- ¼ cup corn flour
- 1 ½ tbsp cinnamon sugar
- ½ cup breadcrumbs

Directions

1. Heat coconut oil in pan over medium heat, add breadcrumbs in pan and stir for 4 minutes. Remove pan from heat and transfer breadcrumbs in bowl.
2. Add almond meal and crush cashew in breadcrumbs and mix well.
3. Peel bananas and cut into half pieces.
4. Dip banana half in corn flour then in beaten egg and finally coat with breadcrumbs.
5. Preheat the air fryer to 360F.
6. Place coated banana in air fryer basket. Sprinkle bananas with cinnamon sugar. Cook for about 10 minutes.
7. Serve and enjoy.

Double Chocolate Chip Cookies

- Ready in 30 minutes
- Servings: 10 cookies

Ingredients

- 1 ¼ cup self-rising flour
- 2/3 cup chocolate chips, any kind or bakers chocolate
- 1/3 cup brown sugar
- ½ cup butter
- 4 tbsp honey
- 1 tbsp milk
- High quality cooking spray

Directions

1. Preheat the air fryer to 320F.
2. In a large bowl cream the butter until it is soft. Add sugar and cream together and blend until they are light and fluffy. Once the mix has reached your desired texture, mix in the honey.
3. Slowly fold in the flour until it has all been added. If you are using baker's chocolate, use a rolling pin to smash it up to give yourself chunks of all different sizes. If you are using chocolate chips, skip this step.
4. Add the chocolate to your cookie dough and blend well so they are evenly distributed throughout the dough.
5. Pour in the milk and thoroughly stir the mixture. Lightly spray your air fryer basket with a cooking spray.
6. Dump or spoon the entire cookie dough mixture into it. Cook the dough for 20 minutes.
7. Cut into 10 portions and serve immediately or store in an air tight container for up to 3 days.

Blueberry Pancakes

- Ready in 20 minutes
- Servings: 2

Ingredients

- ½ tsp vanilla extract
- 2 tbsp honey
- ½ cup blueberries
- ½ cup sugar
- 3 tbsp flour
- 3 eggs, beaten
- 1 cup milk
- 1 tsp baking powder
- A pinch of salt

Directions

1. Preheat the air fryer to 390F.
2. Combine all of the dry ingredients in a large mixing bowl.
3. Add wet ingredients and whisk until the mixture becomes smooth.
4. Stir in blueberries, making sure not to color the dough. You can do that by coating the blueberries with some flour before adding them to the dough.
5. Grease a baking dish. Drop the batter onto the dish, ensuring that the pancakes have some space between them.
6. Do it in two batches if you have too much batter.
7. Bake for about 10 minutes.
8. Serve and enjoy.

Chocolate Molten Lava Cake

- Ready in 25 minutes
- Servings: 2

Ingredients

- 3 ½ oz butter, melted
- 3 ½ tbsp sugar
- 3 ½ ounces chocolate, melted
- 1 cup flour
- 2 large eggs

Directions

1. Preheat the air fryer to 375F.
2. Grease 4 ramekins.
3. In a large bowl beat together the eggs and butter. Stir in the chocolate.
4. Gently fold in the flour.
5. Divide the mixture between the 4 ramekins.
6. Place them in the air fryer and cook for 10 minutes.
7. After 2 minutes, invert them onto serving plates.
8. Enjoy.

Roasted Pumpkin Seeds with Cinnamon

- Ready in 35 minutes
- Servings: 2

Ingredients

- 1 cup pumpkin raw seeds
- 1 tbsp ground cinnamon
- 2 tbsp brown sugar
- 1 cup water
- 1 tbsp olive oil

Directions

1. Add pumpkin seeds, cinnamon and water in a sauté pot. Stir to combine and heat the mixture over high heat. Boil for 2-3 minutes.
2. Drain water and transfer seeds to a kitchen towel. Dry for 20-30 minutes.
3. In the mixing bowl combine sugar, dried seeds, a pinch of cinnamon and 1 tablespoon of olive oil. Mix well.
4. Preheat the Air Fryer to 340F. Transfer seed mixture to the fryer basket. Cook for 15 minutes, shaking couple times. Enjoy.

Apple Wedges with Cinnamon

- Ready in 25 minutes
- Servings: 2

Ingredients

- 2 large apples
- 2 tbsp olive oil
- ½ cup dried apricots, chopped
- 1-2 tbsp brown sugar, to taste
- ½ tsp ground cinnamon

Directions

1. Peel apples and cut each one into quarters. Remove and discard cores. Cut each apple quarter in half to make 2 even wedges (each whole apple is cut into 8 even wedges).
2. Cover apple wedges with the oil.
3. Preheat the air fryer to 350F. Cook apples for about 12-15 minutes, until tender and cooked.
4. Add the apricots and cook for another 3 minutes.
5. Mix together sugar and cinnamon and top cooked apples with the sugar mixture.

Fried Bananas with Ice Cream

- Ready in 25 minutes
- Servings: 2

Ingredients

- 2 large bananas
- 1 tbsp butter
- 1 tbsp brown sugar
- 2 tbsp breadcrumbs
- Vanilla ice cream for serving

Directions

1. Melt butter in the air fryer basket in one minute at 350F.
2. Mix sugar and bread crumbs in a bowl.
3. Cut bananas into 1-inch slices and add to sugar mixture. Mix well.
4. Put covered bananas into air fryer and cook for 10-15 minutes.
5. Serve warm and add ice cream.

Little Apple Pie

- Ready in 30 minutes
- Servings: 1 pie

Ingredients

- 2 large apples
- ½ cup plain flour
- 2 tbsp unsalted butter
- 1 tbsp sugar
- ½ tsp cinnamon

Directions

1. Preheat the Air Fryer to 360F
2. In the large mixing bowl combine flour and butter. Stir to combine. Add sugar and mix well. Add couple tablespoons of water and prepare nice dough. Mix until you get a smooth texture.
3. Take small pastry tins and cover with butter. Fill tins with pastry.
4. Peel and core apples. Dice them. Place diced apples over the pastry and sprinkle with sugar and cinnamon.
5. Transfer pastry tins to an air fryer and cook for 15-17 minutes, until ready.
6. Serve with whipped cream or ice cream.

Chocolate Mug Cake

- Ready in 15 minutes
- Servings: 1 mug cake

Ingredients

- 1 tbsp cocoa powder
- 3 tbsp coconut oil
- ¼ cup self raising flour
- 3 tbsp whole milk
- 5 tbsp powdered sugar

Directions

1. Mix all the ingredients very thoroughly and pour it into not a very tall mug.
2. Preheat the air fryer to 390F.
3. Place the mug into your Air Fryer and set the timer to 10 minutes. Cook until ready and then serve.

Conclusion

Thank you for downloading my book and taking the time to learn new healthy recipes.

I hope that my Air Fryer Cookbook for Two allows you to cook delicious, healthy and low-fat meals. Learn, create and enjoy cooking new interesting meals at home.

Thank you again and be healthy!